Tana Hoban

DIG, DRILL, DUMP, FILL

Greenwillow Books

A DIVISION OF WILLIAM MORROW & COMPANY, INC.
NEW YORK

LIBRARY OF CONGRESS CATALOGING IN PUBLICATION DATA
Hoban, Tana. Dig, drill, dump, fill.
   Summary: Introduces, through photographs alone, heavy construction
machines: earth movers, mixers, diggers, and others.
    1.   Earthmoving machinery—Pictorial works—Juvenile literature.
2.   Construction equipment—Pictorial works—Juvenile literature.
[1.   Earthmoving machinery—Pictorial works.   2.   Construction
equipment—Pictorial works.   3.   Machinery—Pictorial works]
I.   Title.   TA725.H62   624′.152   75-11987
ISBN 0-688-80016-5   ISBN 0-688-84016-7 lib. bdg.

For my sister Freeda

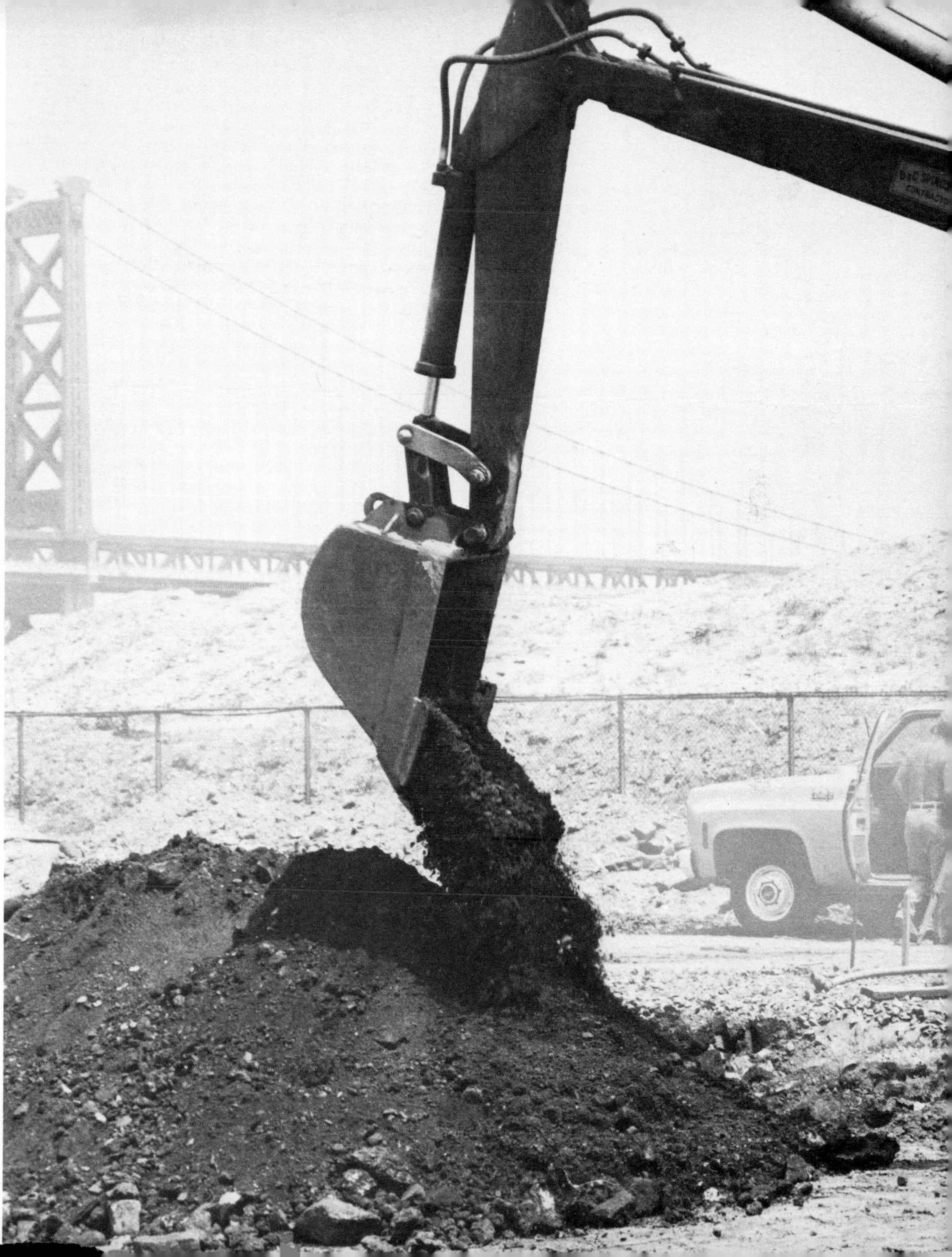

What They Are and What They Do

Many machines get their names from what they do:
a roller rolls, a loader loads, and a dump truck dumps.
Some machines move on rubber tires and go where the
ground is hard or smooth. Some machines move on crawlers
and go where the ground is soft or bumpy.

⌃ **Crawler hydraulic backhoe** digs large ditches and cellars.

⌃ **Crawler front-end loader** scoops and loads rubble and materials to be hauled away. Also digs large holes.

⌃**Paving breaker** cuts, cracks, and crumbles worn-out pavements and streets for repaving.

⌃ **Rubber-tired backhoe and loader** digs small ditches and cellars.

Dump truck hauls and dumps earth, sand, gravel, and rocks.

Concrete truck mixes and hauls concrete.

Crawler crane with clamshell bucket scoops and loads gravel and other materials, digs deep holes, and bites into old buildings for demolition.

Small loader works in tight, small places where a big loader cannot fit. Scoops and unloads.

^ Rubber-tired front-end loader digs and levels gravel, sand, and earth.

^ Crawler crane with electric magnet lifts, sorts, loads, and moves metal.

^ Roller flattens and smooths fresh asphalt.

^Trash truck compresses trash and garbage and hauls it away.

^Street flusher floods and washes the streets with water.